D1567430

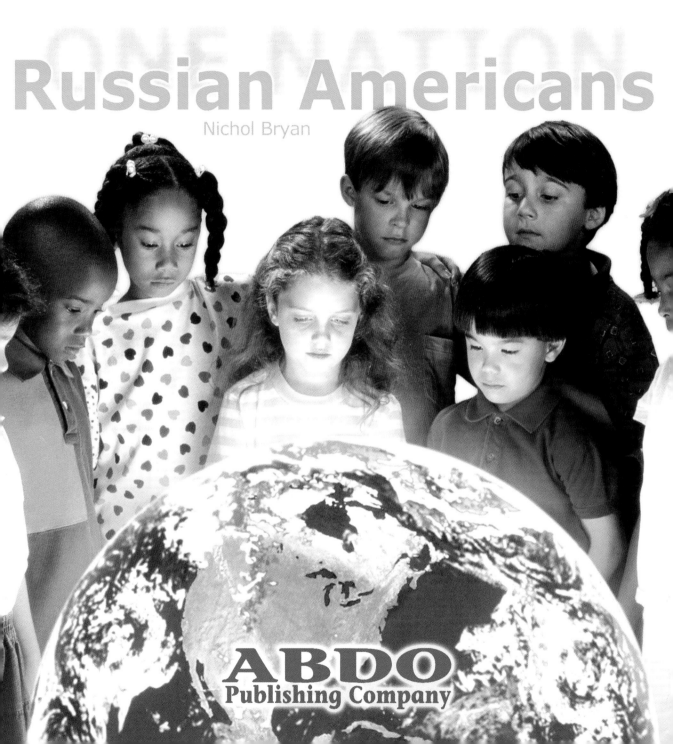

Russian Americans

Nichol Bryan

ABDO
Publishing Company

visit us at
www.abdopub.com

Published by ABDO Publishing Company, 4940 Viking Drive, Edina, Minnesota 55435.
Copyright © 2004 by Abdo Consulting Group, Inc. International copyrights reserved in all countries. No part of this book may be reproduced in any form without written permission from the publisher.

Printed in the United States.

Cover Photo: Corbis
Interior Photos: Corbis pp. 1, 2-3, 5, 7, 9, 10, 11, 12, 14, 19, 22, 23, 24, 25 (bottom), 26, 27, 28, 29, 30-31; Photo Edit pp. 17, 21, 25 (top)

Series Coordinator: Jennifer R. Krueger
Editors: Kristianne E. Buechler, Kate A. Conley
Art Direction & Maps: Neil Klinepier

All of the U.S. population statistics in the One Nation series are taken from the 2000 Census.

Library of Congress Cataloging-in-Publication Data

Bryan, Nichol, 1958-
    Russian Americans / Nichol Bryan.
        p. cm. -- (One nation)
    Summary: Provides information on the history of Russia and on the customs,
language, religion, and experiences of Russian Americans.
    Includes bibliographical references and index.
    ISBN 1-59197-533-6
    1. Russian Americans--Juvenile literature. [1. Russian Americans. 2. Immigrants.] I. Title.

E184.R9B79 2004
973'.049171--dc22

2003066536

Contents

Russian Americans

The Americas were discovered by Christopher Columbus in 1492. He was an Italian explorer working for Spain. Since the age of Columbus, people from around the world have come to America. Most of the first **immigrants** came from Europe.

Immigrants have many reasons for leaving their homes. Some hope to make more money in the United States. They want to send money home to their families in poorer countries. And, some people are not safe in their homeland. They fear **dictators** and military rule. Others flee the instability of revolutions.

Immigrants from Russia have come for all of these reasons. Political and **economic** troubles have driven them from their homes. They seek safety under a new government. They hope to make enough money to support their families. Most of all, they work to form a sense of belonging in their new homeland.

This girl lives in a community of Russian Americans near Homer, Alaska.

Land of the Rus

Russia is the world's largest country. It has an area of more than 6.5 million square miles (17 million sq km). That's almost twice as big as the United States! Russia also has one of the largest populations in the world.

Most Russian people trace their origins to the **Slavs**. The first Slavic state was called Kievan Rus. This state was formed by the Slavs and the **Vikings**. This area became known as "land of the Rus," or Russia.

By 1240, warriors called Mongols had taken over the state. The Mongols appointed princes to rule Russia. These princes gained more and more power. In the late 1400s, a grand prince named Ivan II finally broke Mongol rule. Russia was then ruled by a series of emperors called czars.

Ivan IV was the first Russian leader to be called a czar. He took power in 1533. Ivan IV was also called Ivan the Terrible because he was cruel to his people. The Russians suffered under his rule. He even killed one of his own sons. This first czar died without leaving any children to rule.

Ivan the Terrible's police force often terrorized nobles and peasants.

Life did not improve for many Russians under the reign of the next ruling family. In 1613, Michael Romanov became czar of Russia. The Romanov family ruled the Russian Empire for 300 years.

During this time, most of Russia's peasants lived almost as slaves. Farmers did not own the land they worked. Instead, their lives were controlled by mighty landowners. In the cities, people worked long hours in dangerous factories for little pay.

During the 1700s and 1800s, life was even more uncertain for peasants who were Jewish. The czars encouraged Christians to treat Jews poorly. From time to time, peasants and soldiers attacked Jewish settlements. These attacks were called pogroms.

The early 1900s were also difficult for Russians. During this time, Russia fought on the same side as the United States in **World War I**. Many people were out of work and could not afford food. These conditions led to a revolution headed by Vladimir Lenin. The revolution ended Romanov rule in 1917.

The revolutionaries declared a **communist** government. Lenin became the government's leader. In 1922, Russia and three other republics formed the Union of Soviet Socialist Republics. It was also called the Soviet Union. Over time, it grew to include 15 republics.

The Romanov children pose for a portrait around 1910, shortly before the communists took over.

The Soviet Union's **communist** rulers promised to make all Russians equal. They would run the factories and farms for the benefit of everyone. It didn't work out that way, however. Members of the ruling party grew rich and powerful. But, many citizens of the Soviet Union, including Russians, remained poor.

Lenin died in 1924. Another **communist**, Joseph Stalin, then ruled the Soviet Union until 1953. During Stalin's rule, government-controlled industries and farms did not provide enough goods for everyone. People had to wait in line for hours to get food or clothing.

The government also did not allow freedom of religion. Independent political parties were outlawed. People who spoke out against the government were sent to **labor camps**. Millions of Russians suspected of disloyalty were starved, tortured, and killed.

Mikhail Gorbachev

During **World War II**, the United States and the Soviet Union were **allies**. But after the war, the United States and the Soviet Union both wanted to influence other countries. This period was called the **Cold War**.

Mikhail Gorbachev became the leader of the Soviet Union in 1985. He wanted to create a more fair and **democratic** country. In 1991, this led to the collapse of the Soviet Union and the end of the Cold War. Russia's people finally had democratically elected leaders. They also had liberties such as freedom of religion.

After the collapse of the Soviet Union, relations with other countries remained tense. However, Vladimir Putin worked to change that after Russians elected him president in 2000. He has also worked to improve the Russian **economy**.

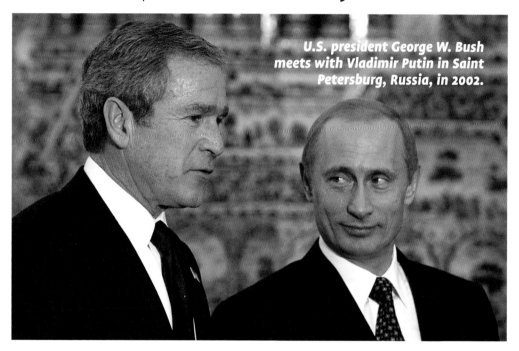

U.S. president George W. Bush meets with Vladimir Putin in Saint Petersburg, Russia, in 2002.

Some people are now able to start their own businesses and make a better life. Many Russians, however, are even poorer than they had been under the Soviets. But, the people of Russia continue to work to support their families in an improving economy.

Leaving Russia

The first Russians to settle in what is now the United States were fur traders. In the mid-1700s, they crossed the narrow Bering Strait. They wanted to hunt and trap in present-day Alaska. At the time, this land was a remote part of the Russian Empire.

Over the next century, other Russians followed. They came mostly to escape religious or ethnic **persecution** under the czars. They hoped for peace and freedom.

Russia sold Alaska to the United States in 1867. Many of the Russians in Alaska returned to Russia. But, some stayed and became Russian Americans.

Oppression continued to drive Russians to America. In the 1880s, thousands of Russian Jews came to the United States. They were coming to escape the pogroms.

Sitka, Alaska, was a bustling fur-trading town used by both Russians and Americans in the late 1800s.

Russian **immigrants** arriving in America in the late 1800s were often from farms or villages. They had to adjust to living in the larger cities of the United States. Many settled in New York City, the port of entry for millions of immigrants.

The Journey from Russia to the United States

New York's Lower East Side in 1910

Many Russian Jews settled in New York City's Lower East Side. They formed a community with other Jewish **immigrants** from eastern Europe. Other Russian Jews settled in different cities, such as Los Angeles and Seattle. There, they began new Russian-American communities.

More Russians fled to America after the **communist** revolution in 1917. Some of these were members of wealthy families. They had controlled much of Russia's land under the czars. Others came to escape the instability that gripped Russia after the revolution.

These immigrants often faced **discrimination** in the United States. Because Russia was communist, some Americans suspected that Russian immigrants were planning to overthrow the U.S. government. The U.S. Justice Department arrested many Russians for this reason. Most were released, but some were sent back to Russia.

Russian-American Communities

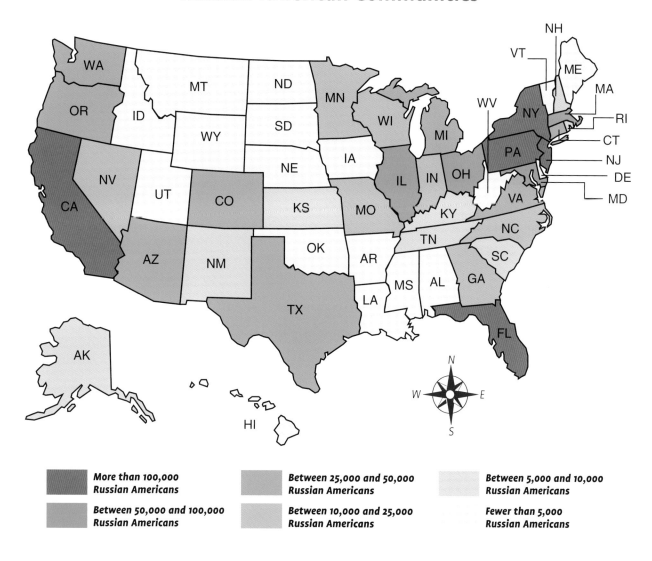

More than 100,000 Russian Americans	Between 25,000 and 50,000 Russian Americans	Between 5,000 and 10,000 Russian Americans
Between 50,000 and 100,000 Russian Americans	Between 10,000 and 25,000 Russian Americans	Fewer than 5,000 Russian Americans

Becoming a Russian American grew even more difficult during **World War II**. Russians were not allowed to travel freely during this time. From 1930 to 1944, only around 14,000 Russians **immigrated** to America. However, many more tried.

During the **Cold War**, Russians were still not allowed to travel freely. Immigration laws in the United States were also strictly enforced. Few were able to escape Russia.

But, some did manage to gain **asylum** in the United States. These people were looking for greater freedom. They included Russian Jews and others who were **persecuted** by the **communists**. Many were highly educated scientists, writers, athletes, and artists.

Russians were finally free to leave their country after the end of the Cold War in 1991. Thousands came to the United States. The new Russian immigrants were coming for better jobs and a better life.

Today, Russia is a modern, industrial nation. The Russians who come to America now are different from those who came a century ago. Now, most people come from cities rather than farms. They often have a high school or university education.

The Soviet government used to emphasize science and technology. So, many Russian **immigrants** have been trained as physicists, engineers, doctors, and technical professionals. Now, many Russian immigrants own their own business in the United States.

This Russian-American couple owns a deli in Los Angeles, California.

Becoming a Citizen

Russians and other **immigrants** who come to the United States take the same path to citizenship. Immigrants become citizens in a process called naturalization. A government agency called the United States Citizenship and Immigration Services (USCIS) oversees this process.

The Path to Citizenship

Applying for Citizenship

The first step in becoming a citizen is filling out a form. It is called the Application for Naturalization. On the application, immigrants provide information about their past. Immigrants send the application to the USCIS.

Providing Information

Besides the application, immigrants must provide the USCIS with other items. They may include documents such as marriage licenses or old tax returns. Immigrants must also provide photographs and fingerprints. They are used for identification. The fingerprints are also used to check whether immigrants have committed crimes in the past.

The Interview

Next, a USCIS officer interviews each immigrant to discuss his or her application and background. In addition, the USCIS officer tests the immigrant's ability to speak, read, and write in English. The officer also tests the immigrant's knowledge of American civics.

The Oath

Immigrants approved for citizenship must take the Oath of Allegiance. Once immigrants take this oath, they are citizens. During the oath, immigrants promise to renounce loyalty to their native country, to support the U.S. Constitution, and to serve and defend the United States when needed.

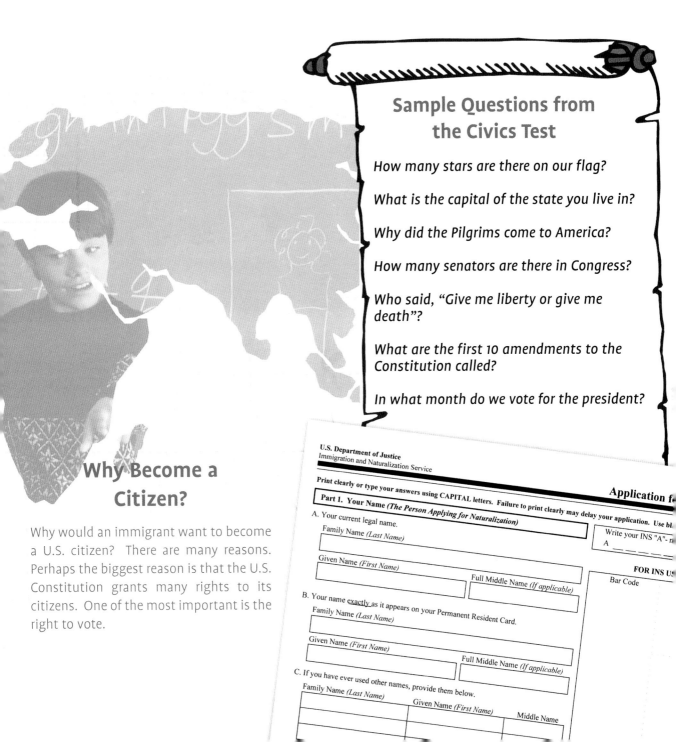

Sample Questions from the Civics Test

How many stars are there on our flag?

What is the capital of the state you live in?

Why did the Pilgrims come to America?

How many senators are there in Congress?

Who said, "Give me liberty or give me death"?

What are the first 10 amendments to the Constitution called?

In what month do we vote for the president?

Why Become a Citizen?

Why would an immigrant want to become a U.S. citizen? There are many reasons. Perhaps the biggest reason is that the U.S. Constitution grants many rights to its citizens. One of the most important is the right to vote.

U.S. Department of Justice
Immigration and Naturalization Service

Print clearly or type your answers using CAPITAL letters. Failure to print clearly may delay your application. Use bl

Application f

Part 1. Your Name *(The Person Applying for Naturalization)*

A. Your current legal name.

Family Name *(Last Name)*

Given Name *(First Name)*

Full Middle Name *(If applicable)*

Write your INS "A"- n

A _ _ _ _ _

FOR INS U

Bar Code

B. Your name exactly as it appears on your Permanent Resident Card.

Family Name *(Last Name)*

Given Name *(First Name)*

Full Middle Name *(If applicable)*

C. If you have ever used other names, provide them below.

Family Name *(Last Name)*

Given Name *(First Name)*

Middle Name

American Life

Some Russian **immigrants** tell stories of how difficult their lives were in Russia. It is no surprise that many Russian Americans are happy to live in the United States. They have blended much of their **culture** with American ways. They have created a culture that is **uniquely** Russian American.

Bounty of the Fields

Grains and potatoes are usually the primary source of food for peasants and city dwellers alike in Russia. Grain dishes such as bread pancakes, puddings, and **pastries** are popular. Meat stews and seafood are also eaten. Russian Americans still enjoy these dishes in their new home.

Today, many Russian Americans eat at restaurants that serve Russian food. These have also become popular with other Americans. And, Russian Americans can buy special ingredients in many cities that have Russian food stores.

Opposite page: Russian Americans can find foods from their homeland in Russian-owned restaurants like this one in Brooklyn, New York.

Russian-American Families

In Russia, many people lived in large, extended families. They lived with their parents, children, grandparents, aunts, and uncles. Often, they all lived in the same house.

Russians who came to the United States during the Soviet era struggled to keep their families together. But this was very difficult. Not all Russians were allowed to emigrate freely. Today, Russian-American families value the time they spend together.

Some Russian Americans continue the tradition of living with their extended family.

Ancient Faiths

Most Russians, and many Russian Americans, are members of the Russian Orthodox Church. Many other Russian Americans are Jewish. Some Russian Americans follow other faiths or are not religious.

Under Soviet rule, religion of any type was harshly restricted. This is one reason why some Russian Americans practice no religion. But, many are trying to rediscover the religions of their ancestors. Others are adopting new faiths in their new homeland.

Many beautiful Russian Orthodox churches, such as this one in Alaska, were built in Russian-American communities.

A World Language

Most Russian people speak the Russian language. Russian was also taught in schools in other countries controlled by the Soviet Union. As a result, more than 158 million people in many countries now speak Russian as their first language.

Learning English has always been one of the biggest challenges for Russians coming to America. This is partly because they must learn a new alphabet. Russian uses an alphabet called Cyrillic. This is different from the Latin alphabet used in English.

The Cyrillic alphabet can be seen in this carved wood and bone panel that was created in the 1700s.

Signs in Russian are a common sight in Russian-American communities such as Brighton Beach, New York.

The Cyrillic Alphabet

The Cyrillic alphabet can look confusing to English speakers. It looks like a mix of familiar letters such as A and B with strange symbols such as ф and Γ. The alphabet was developed in the 800s and 900s.

Heritage

Russian music, ballet, theater, drama, and literature are widely considered the finest in the world. Russian Americans brought this heritage with them to America.

Igor Stravinsky

For example, Igor Stravinsky was a Russian American who composed music for many famous ballets. These include *The Firebird* and *The Rite of Spring*. He lived in many countries in Europe and finally came to America in 1940. He became an American citizen in 1945.

A Russian American who brought the **culture** of ballet to America was Alexandra Danilova. She was one of the world's greatest ballerinas. She left Russia in the 1920s and toured the world with ballet companies. Then, she came to teach dance at the School of American Ballet. She became an American citizen in 1946.

Another talented Russian-American woman was Natalie Wood. She was an actress born of Russian parents in San Francisco. She starred in many famous films, such as *Rebel Without a Cause* and *West Side Story*. Although her parents could barely speak English, she became one of the most famous American film stars in history.

Natalie Wood's real name, Natasha Nikolaevna Gurdin, sounds much more Russian than her stage name.

David Sarnoff was also a pioneer of radio broadcasting.

Some of the most important discoveries in physics, psychology, and space flight were also made by Russian scientists. Russian American scientists and engineers have helped America remain the world's technological leader.

One Russian-American scientist was Vladimir Zworykin. He pioneered the development of television. He invented and patented the idea of color television in 1928. Another Russian American, David Sarnoff, created the world's first broadcasting network in 1926. Today, it is still called the National Broadcasting Company, or NBC.

The Russian people have faced many hardships and tragedies in their long history. Yet, Russian Americans have overcome the suffering in their homeland. They have also overcome the mistrust of others in America. They have added their rich heritage, strong work ethic, and determination to America's **culture**.

Vladimir Zworykin holds the cathode-ray tube. It is an important part of his invention, the television.

Glossary

allies - people or countries that agree to help each other in times of need. During World War II, Great Britain, France, the United States, and the Soviet Union were called the Allies.

asylum - protection in another country from persecution in a person's home country.

Cold War - a period of tension and hostility between the United States and its allies and the Soviet Union and its allies after World War II.

communism - a social and economic system in which everything is owned by the government and is distributed to the people as needed.

culture - the customs, arts, and tools of a nation or people at a certain time.

democracy - a governmental system in which the people vote on how to run their country.

dictator - a ruler with complete control who usually governs in a cruel or unfair way.

discrimination - unfair treatment based on factors such as a person's race, religion, or gender.

economy - the way a nation uses its money, goods, and natural resources.

immigration - entry into another country to live. A person who immigrates is called an immigrant.

labor camp - a place where people are forced to work against their will.

oppress - to control with unfair force and cruelty.

pastry - a sweet, baked food.

persecution - harassment due to one's origin, religion, or other beliefs.

Slav - a member of a group of people who speak similar languages and live in eastern and central Europe.

unique - being the only one of its kind.

Viking - a member of a group of warrior explorers who came from Scandinavia.

World War I - from 1914 to 1918, fought in Europe. The United States, Great Britain, France, Russia, and their allies were on one side. Germany, Austria-Hungary, and their allies were on the other side.

World War II - from 1939 to 1945, fought in Europe, Asia, and Africa. The United States, France, Great Britain, the Soviet Union, and their allies were on one side. Germany, Italy, Japan, and their allies were on the other side.

Saying It

Cyrillic - suh-RIH-lihk
czar - ZAHR
Igor Stravinsky - EE-guhr struh-VIHN-skee
Kievan Rus - kee-EH-vahn ROOS
Mikhail Gorbachev - mee-KILE gawr-buh-CHAWF
Vladimir Lenin - VLAD-uh-mihr LEHN-uhn
Vladimir Putin - VLAD-uh-mihr POO-tuhn
Vladimir Zworykin - VLAD-uh-mihr ZVAWR-kyihn

Web Sites

To learn more about Russian Americans, visit ABDO Publishing Company on the World Wide Web at **www.abdopub.com**. Web sites about Russian Americans are featured on our Book Links page. These links are routinely monitored and updated to provide the most current information available.

Index